The Story of Persephone

Penelope Farmer

ILLUSTRATED BY

Graham McCallum

WILLIAM MORROW AND COMPANY

NEW YORK 1973

Persephone was Demeter's only child. She and the goddess of the corn harvest were more like sisters, like lovers even, than a mother and a daughter, wandering the hills together through a world which saw no winter, no autumn, no death or decay, only spring and summer, birth and harvest. Wherever they wandered flowers sprang up, spring flowers for Persephone, summer flowers for the goddess Demeter.

Persephone grew up beautiful, as beautiful as her mother but cool and pale like spring, whereas Demeter was warm and golden like the ripened corn. Men who saw Persephone now desired her, wanted to take her from her mother's side. But Persephone clung to Demeter tearfully, and Demeter sent away each man in turn.

So they remained together, mother and daughter, Persephone everything to Demeter, Demeter everything to Persephone. And they were happy. But the happiness of gods is as fragile as the happiness of men. Hades, god of the Underworld, caught sight of Persephone and he, too, fell passionately in love. He risked no refusal as his rivals had. Obsessed by Persephone, determined to have her, he watched continually, invisible. A black rock, a hawthorn tree, a cloud on the hillside, Hades spied on Demeter and Persephone, until at last one day the daughter wandered from the mother, careless, happy, unthinking of danger.

The valley was empty, except for goats grazing peacefully in a field of wild narcissi. But then Hades erupted from the earth. His golden fiery chariot was drawn by four black horses that tossed their heads and reared and screamed

when they heard the screams of Persephone. Hades ignored her fear, seized her, lifted her into his chariot. He whipped up his horses, calling on the earth, which at once gaped obediently, greedily swallowing them. Horses, chariot, Hades, Persephone vanished from the sight of men, from the eye of Helios, the golden sun.

The goats fell helpless, too, into the open void before it closed again. Then the torn earth healed itself. Flowers grew peacefully as if they had never been disturbed. When Demeter in her turn came across the hill, the valley was calm once more, unwounded, but it was empty. Persephone had gone.

Demeter ran over the hills, calling out her name. Persephone! At first playfully, then anxiously, at last grief stricken, desperate: Persephone!

Birds rose startled from their nests. Animals ran for cover. Small sounds and movements filled the hills and valleys as the earth responded to the goddess's cries. But no sound, no movement revealed Persephone.

Demeter stood like a statue, weeping. Her golden beauty faded in a little while. Sorrow withered her into a bent old woman, just as summer declines through autumn into winter—even her clothes grew ragged like autumn leaves. She wandered the world in search of Persephone, but no one recognized her as a goddess now. Men treated her as a beggar woman, well or ill. Some, respecting her age and pitying her poverty, took her in and sat her by their hearths and fed her generously. Others let her shelter in their stables and gave her husks to eat as if she were a sow. Some drove her from their doors with shouts or blows.

"Have you seen a girl, dark-haired, pale, as beautiful as spring?"

While Demeter cursed the cruel and blessed the kind, from cruel and kind alike she asked for news of Persephone. But all said no, they had not heard of her.

Then Demeter at last resumed her goddess's form and joined her fellow gods on Mount Olympus. For Persephone might have caught the fancy of some god. Great Zeus himself had stolen many women in his time. But Zeus swore he knew nothing of Persephone.

Demeter asked Hades himself, white-faced, black-clad, the god of the Underworld, who stared her coldly in the eye and denied all knowledge of her daughter. Even on Olympus among his fellow gods, his breath felt chilly to the flesh and smelled of lilies, flowers of death.

"Ask Helios, Demeter," advised the witch-goddess Hecate, who sat near Hades on Olympus. "The sun sees everything. He may have seen your daughter's fate."

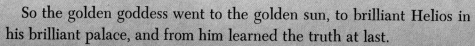

So the golden goddess went to the golden sun, to brilliant Helios in his brilliant palace, and from him learned the truth at last.

"I saw Hades steal Persephone. Scream as she might, he snatched her from the earth and took her down into the Underworld. Now she rules there as his queen."

Demeter's grief turned immediately to rage, making her terrible. Shrieking, she swept across the world, while the earth shriveled and died behind her, more devastated than if by fire or storm. Crops were flattened, flowers withered, fruit rotted on the trees. The air was filled with cries and wails as children grew thinner, starved, and died. Their parents wept for them as Demeter wept for Persephone.

Men, despairing, prayed to the gods for help. Some poured libations to the great god Zeus and begged for him to pity them.

"If the earth will not support us, we shall starve and die. Already the women are weeping for our children."

Mighty Zeus called Hades and Demeter before him now and spoke with dignity.

"The earth must bear fruit again. You, Demeter, must contain your grief. But if Persephone has not eaten of the food of the dead, you, Hades, must restore her to her mother, Demeter."

Then Hades led Demeter to his kingdom of the shades, the Underworld, across the river Styx, rowed by Charon the ferryman, through the asphodel fields, to Erebus. His palace stood among cypress groves beside the pool of Lethe, and there between pillars of silver and black sat his queen, Persephone.

She was as beautiful as she had ever been, but her beauty was wintry now, no longer the beauty of spring. She wore a black dress and sat on a black throne. Her face did not move or change as she saw her mother come. The hand she gave Demeter felt as cold, as unyielding, as ice.

The hall was thronged with the shadows of the dead, who stirred and murmured when they heard Demeter's voice.

"Have you eaten in Hades, Persephone? Have you eaten the food of the dead?"

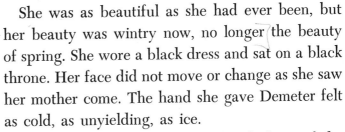

Still Persephone did not speak, but pointed to a dish filled with withered fruit, apples, peaches, pomegranates. Their skin was hard and dark and dry, as if caught by frost or swept by fire, like the fruit on earth destroyed by Demeter's fury.

Hades stood on the steps of his throne. He demanded of the shadows watching him, "Has anything in the Underworld passed Persephone's lips?" The shades stirred again, but all were silent still. "Has Persephone eaten of the food of the dead?"

"No one answers. Then, Hades, I shall take my daughter."

The shadows moved aside from Demeter's path as she led Persephone from the hall. But when she reached the threshold, one shade stepped out and barred her way—so small, so insignificant a shade, the goddess at first ignored him.

He raised his voice and hooted derisively, "I saw Queen Persephone eat: five pomegranate seeds."

If Demeter heard, she did not seem to understand his words at once. The shade cried again triumphantly, "I alone saw her eat those seeds." And Persephone heard and understood. Her mother saw the frozen tears run slowly down her face. And when she looked back toward Hades' throne, she saw Hades, smiling, take from the dish of fruit a pomegranate, brown and withered as the rest. He held it up so that all the hall could see. One side was opened; five seeds had gone.

Demeter let fall her daughter's hand, let Hades lead his queen back to her wintry throne. She cursed the shade who had betrayed Persephone and turned him into an owl to hoot forever among the cypress groves. Then alone, dry-eyed, she left the Underworld.

She raged no more. Her rage had died, turned to cold despair. She shut herself away, and the world without her froze, became as black and cold and barren as the lands of the farthest north. Animals crept into holes to die. Birds pecked uselessly at earth hard as iron. Men, women, children starved and died, too wretched even to pray to the gods for help.

But Zeus saw and pitied them. He called Hades and Demeter before him once more, and again he sat in judgment, severe and terrible, his face stormy, his eyes flashing fire.

"Do you want between you to destroy the world I made? I make my edict now, and you must obey. For each of the five pomegranate seeds Demeter's daughter shall spend one month each year with Hades in the Underworld. The seven months remaining she shall spend with you, Demeter, upon earth. Go, Hades, restore Persephone to her mother's side."

Demeter waited in the valley from which Hades had snatched Persephone. The earth was cold now, without grass or flowers, the hillside bare rock. The earth opened. Persephone rising from it, frozen-

eyed, was pale as from the tomb. But Demeter took her in her arms, and as she kissed her the color came back into Persephone's cheeks. Her eyes began to take life again.

Just so the earth began to blossom. A skin of grass crept over the bare soil. Plants grew, budded, burst into flower. Leaves covered the trees, and the crops sprang up in the fields. The world flourished as it used to do.

After seven months, the crops of fruit and corn being safely gathered in, men with full bellies gave thanks to the gods. Children looked fat and well again and laughed instead of cried.

But then Hades, returning in his chariot, took Persephone with him to the Underworld, and then Demeter sorrowed for her again. The fruits and flowers withered, the world died. Yet all the time beneath the soil the seeds of new plants waited, tended by Persephone in the Underworld, until it was her time to return to earth again.

So, yearly, Persephone returns to her mother and leaves her. Season follows season: spring, summer, autumn, winter. The earth blossoms and dies alternately as Demeter rejoices and Demeter weeps.